All Kinds of Friends

My Friend Uses a Wheelchair

by Kirsten Chang

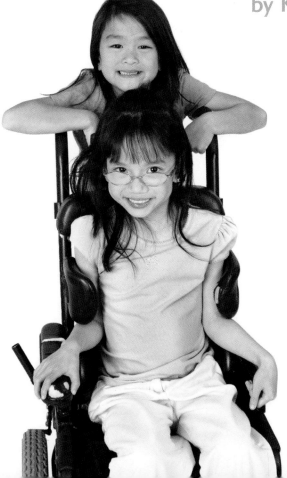

Bullfrog Books

Ideas for Parents and Teachers

Bullfrog Books let children practice reading informational text at the earliest reading levels. Repetition, familiar words, and photo labels support early readers.

Before Reading
- Discuss the cover photo. What does it tell them?

- Look at the picture glossary together. Read and discuss the words.

Read the Book
- "Walk" through the book and look at the photos. Let the child ask questions. Point out the photo labels.

- Read the book to the child, or have him or her read independently.

After Reading
- Prompt the child to think more. Ask: Do you know someone who uses a wheelchair? How can you be a good friend to him or her?

Bullfrog Books are published by Jump!
5357 Penn Avenue South
Minneapolis, MN 55419
www.jumplibrary.com

Library of Congress Cataloging-in-Publication Data

Names: Chang, Kirsten, 1991– author.
Title: My friend uses a wheelchair / by Kirsten Chang.
Description: Minneapolis, MN: Bullfrog Books, Jump!, [2020] | Series: All kinds of friends Includes bibliographical references and index.
Identifiers: LCCN 2018050525 (print)
LCCN 2018053982 (ebook)
ISBN 9781641287401 (ebook)
ISBN 9781641287388 (hardcover : alk. paper)
ISBN 9781641287395 (pbk.)
Subjects: LCSH: Children with disabilities—Juvenile literature. | Wheelchairs—Juvenile literature.
Classification: LCC HV903 (ebook)
LCC HV903 .C43 2020 (print) | DDC 305.9/08083—dc23
LC record available at https://lccn.loc.gov/2018050525

Editor: Susanne Bushman
Designer: Molly Ballanger

Photo Credits: Tad Saddoris, cover, 8, 9 (foreground), 23br; ktaylorg/iStock, 1, 24; Image Source/iStock, 3; fatihhoca/iStock, 4, 5, 6–7; bearmoney/Shutterstock, 9 (background); AnnGaysorn/Shutterstock, 10–11 (boy), 12–13, 23tr; CHUYN/iStock, 10–11 (ramp), 23tr; Zoja Hussainova/Shuttestock, 14–15, 23bl; Jaren Jai Wicklund/Shutterstock, 16; Richard Hutchings/Getty, 17; FatCamera/iStock, 18–19; kali9/iStock, 20–21; Vereshchagin Dmitry/Shutterstock, 22; dnaveh/Shutterstock, 23tl.

Printed in the United States of America at Corporate Graphics in North Mankato, Minnesota.

Table of Contents

Wheels Are Fun

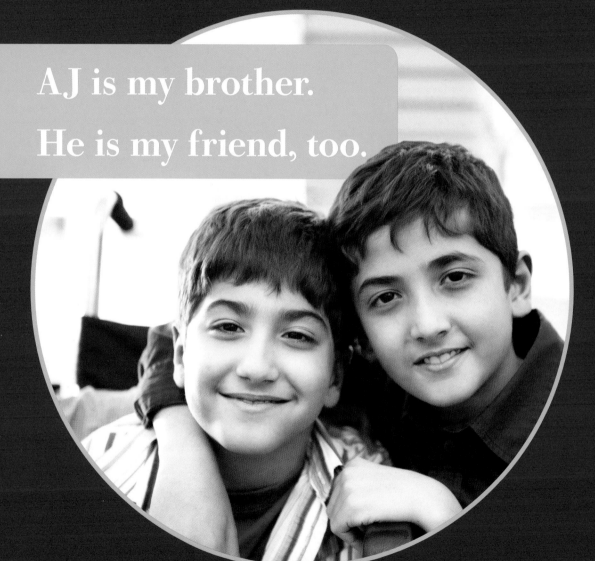

AJ is my brother.
He is my friend, too.

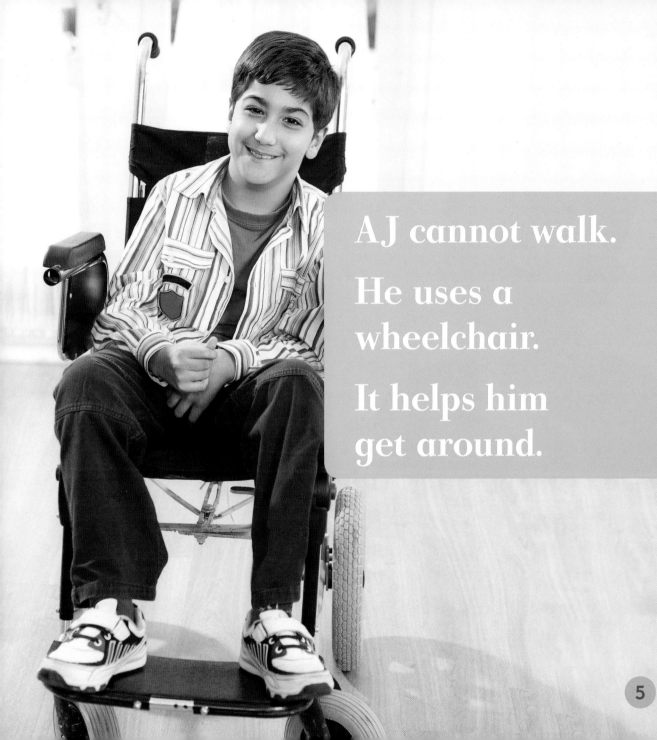

AJ cannot walk.

He uses a wheelchair.

It helps him get around.

We play music.
We have fun!

Sam was injured.
She cannot
walk anymore.

Now she uses
a wheelchair.

She still loves to paint.

Jay goes to the beach.

He uses a ramp.

ramp

Jay gets out of
his wheelchair.

Dad helps him.

They play in the sand.

Fun!

Tim and Jo dance.
They make a routine.
Cool!

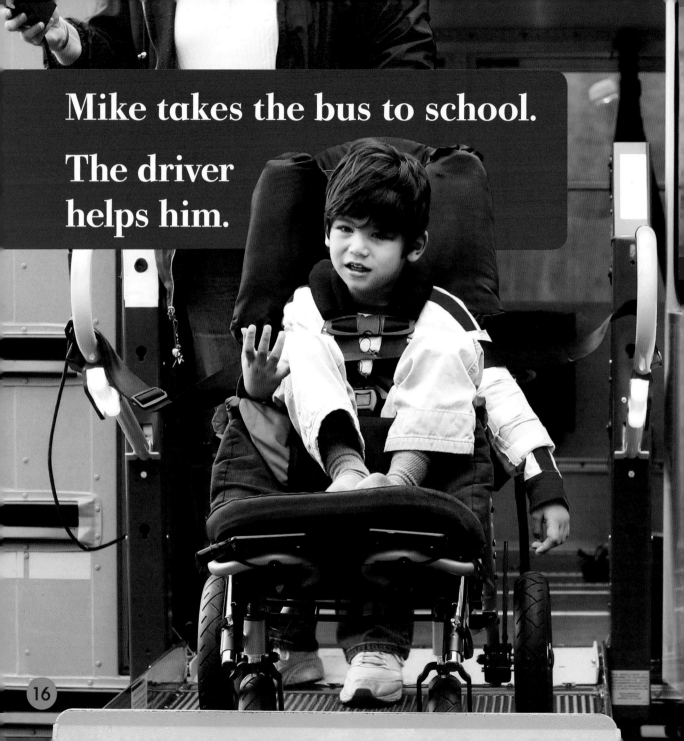

Mike takes the bus to school.
The driver helps him.

Cal's mom brings him.
I ask if I can help.
I like to help!

ramp

17

Anna plays sports.
I cheer her on.
Go, Anna!

Wheelchairs do not stop my friends.

They can do many things!

Parts of a Wheelchair

There are different kinds of wheelchairs. This one has a motor! See the rest of its parts.

headrest

controller

backrest

footrest

motor

wheel

Picture Glossary

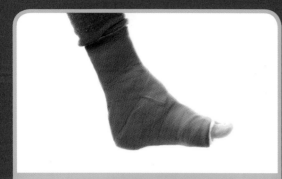

injured
Hurt or damaged.

ramp
A slope that connects two different levels.

routine
A planned set of movements.

wheelchair
A chair with wheels that is used by people who cannot walk or have difficulty walking.

Index

To Learn More

Finding more information is as easy as 1, 2, 3.

❶ Go to www.factsurfer.com

❷ Enter "myfriendusesawheelchair" into the search box.

❸ Choose your book to see a list of websites.